The Cyclic System of Transposition for Trumpet

The Cyclic System of Transposition for Trumpet

Lenard C. Bowie, DMA

ILLUSTRATIONS BY KEITH DOLES
EDITED BY PATRICE L. BOWIE

Copyright © 2014 by Lenard C. Bowie, DMA.

Library of Congress Control Number: 2013923330
ISBN: Softcover   978-1-4931-5551-4
         eBook   978-1-4931-5552-1

All rights reserved. No part of this book may be reproduced or transmitted in any form or by any means, electronic or mechanical, including photocopying, recording, or by any information storage and retrieval system, without permission in writing from the copyright owner.

This book was printed in the United States of America.

Rev. date: 12/30/2013

To order additional copies of this book, contact:
Xlibris LLC
1-888-795-4274
www.Xlibris.com
Orders@Xlibris.com
144531

Contents

What is Transposition? 9
Principles of the Cyclic System 13

    Parallel Keys 15
    Reading Upper Parallel Keys 17
    Reading Lower Parallel Keys 19
    Reading Neighboring Keys 21
    Reading in "C" Clefs 23
    Reading F Clefs 25

Determining the Interval of Transposition (Iot) 27
Transposition Chart for Commonly Used Trumpets 29
Applying the Cyclic System of Transposition 31
Interpreting Alterations 39
Perfecting the Cyclic System 41
Subject Index 43

Introduction

The study of transposition is of great importance to prospective composers, arrangers, conductors and performance majors studying orchestral instruments. This is due to the fact that the subject is central to the content of almost every performance-oriented course in the collegiate instrumental music curriculum.

Having witnessed the level of frustration and confusion suffered by most neophyte trumpet students, and finally admitting my own ineptness with the subject, I started an in depth study of transposition over thirty years ago with the intent of resolving my own misconceptions about the subject. This study led to the development of a system of transposition that I could easily understand—one that would apply to all trumpets and would answer all of my questions pertaining to transposition.

My study revealed the following factors as root causes of my misconceptions about transposition. In subsequent years, I found these same factors to be the cause of frustration and misconception for the average student regarding the subject of transposition; specifically:

1. The misconception that *instruments* transpose.
2. The misunderstanding about the differences between **"written"** and **"sounding" pitch.**

3. Transposition is ***defined*** and ***approached*** differently by teachers who specialize in different music disciplines.
4. For most music students and professionals, transposition is regarded as a **"theoretical"** process. For the prospective and professional orchestral trumpeter, transposition is a *performance skill*, of which mastery is ultimately required.

To confirm the level of confusion on the subject of transposition, one has only to google "Trumpet Transposition" to be confronted with a number of different methods and approaches used by professional musicians, and some of their confusion about the subject. *The Cyclic System of Transposition for Trumpet* incorporates the more salient approaches and concepts of transposition systems that can be used effectively for any pitched trumpet.

Lenard C. Bowie, DMA

WHAT IS TRANSPOSITION?

Simply stated, transposition is the mental skill or theoretical process of reading or writing music in a key different from the one indicated on the printed page. The process of transposition also involves reading pitches in an octave other than the one indicated.

This definition revolves around several questions, the answers to which are essential for understanding and developing the skills essential to the process of transposing. The questions, in specific, are:

1. **What is the difference between "written" and "sounding" pitch?**
   Written pitch is a set of graphic symbols indicated on paper or other surface, or pitch images perceived in the mind. Written pitch can only be *seen* or *imagined*, but cannot be *heard*. On the other hand, sounding pitch is the actual audible image produced by an instrument. Sounding pitch can only be heard or imagined, but cannot be "seen".

2. **Why do instruments transpose?**
   Instruments *do* *not* transpose—**people** transpose. Specifically, trumpets are designed acoustically and physically to produce pitches consistent with their physical dimensions and properties (length, bore size, shape, i.e.,

conical or cylindrical). When supplied with an appropriate amount of air pressure, the instrument will sound pitches consistent with the natural harmonics produced by those specific dimensions of length and size. Once produced, those sounds may be modified or changed by the use of valves, slides, keys or changes in air pressure. In other words, transposition is not a process of "blowing" a specific pitch into the mouthpiece end of the instrument and getting a totally different pitch from the bell end. The output of sound at the bell end of the instrument is consistent with the input of air volume or pressure into the mouthpiece end of the instrument, in conjunction with its physical dimensions and properties.

3. **If instruments do not transpose, why do people transpose?**
People transpose as a matter of efficiency or convenience. To facilitate the teaching and learning of several different pitched instruments of the same family, it is more efficient or practical to use the same fingerings to produce the same written notes. Otherwise, it would be necessary for each instrument of the same family, of a different pitch, to use a different set of fingerings to produce the same written notes. However, it should be noted that tubas, for instance, are considered to be "non-transposing" or "concert pitched" instruments, with each differently pitched tuba sounding the same pitches as those written, yet each of the variously pitched tubas must use a unique set of fingerings to achieve the respective pitches written for each such tuba.

4. **What are so-called "transposing instruments"?**
   a. Any treble clef instrument that has a pitch designation other than "C", is considered to be a
   transposing instrument, i.e., trumpets in F, Bb, Eb, D, etc.

b. Any instrument which sound pitches other than those written for it, regardless of its clef or pitch designation. For example, the woodwind piccolo in C and the string bass are considered as concert pitched or non-transposing instruments. However, since they sound an octave above or below their respective written notations, it is realistic to classify them as "transposing instruments".

5. What are so-called "non-transposing instruments"?
Excepting those instruments indicated in previous explanations, non-transposing or concert pitched instruments are those having a pitch designation of "C" or no pitch designation at all, i.e., piano, violin, 'cello, etc. These instruments sound the same pitches in the range written for them.

It is common for arrangers and composers to specify trumpets of various pitches in their works. Since there is a trumpet representative of each of the thirteen (13) pitches of the chromatic scale, it is not practical to own all 13 of them. Therefore, it is necessary for trumpeters to learn the skill of transposing to compensate for the instruments they do not own or have access to. The methods most commonly used to transpose have a number of advantages as well as disadvantages. These transposition techniques include:

   a) Reading notation in lesser known clefs.
   b) Looking at one note, while thinking of, or reading another note.
   c) Negotiating the problem of alterations in chromatic music.

Principles of the Cyclic System

The transposition system described herein is built from the more advantageous and prominent features of the above three transposition techniques. The "cyclic system" employs three basic skills, that when expanded and superimposed one on the other, *revolves* through every pitch and key in tonal music—hence the title of this book: *The Cyclic System of Transposition for Trumpet.* The three basic skills of this system are:

1. Read in **"Parallel"** Keys
    a. Upper Parallel-Read a half-step above the written key and notation.
    b. Lower Parallel-Read a half-step below the written key and notation.
2. Read in **"Neighboring"** Keys
    a. Upper Neighbor-Read a whole step above the written key and notation.
    b. Read a whole step below the written key and notation.
    c. Read the written notation in C or alto clef.
3. Read in **F Clefs**
    a. Read the original treble clef notation in bass clef.
    b. Read the original treble clef notation in baritone clef.

PARALLEL KEYS

Music written in the Western Hemisphere consists of seven prime or key notes, through which all musical thought is expressed: A, B, C, D, E, F, and G. These seven notes maintain their alphabetical identity and sequential order in a diatonic, chromatic or arpeggiated configuration, regardless of direction, (ascending or descending), relationship to key (root, third, fifth, etc.), or the extent of alteration (i.e., whether CX, C#, C, Cb or Cbb—they are all C's). Therefore, parallel keys are derived from opposite ends of an eight note cycle above or below the prime or key note.

LOWER PARALLEL KEYS	KEY NOTES	UPPER PARALLEL KEYS
B♭	B	B# (or C♮**)
A♭ (G#)	A	A# (or B♭**)
G♭ (F#)	G	G# (or A♭**)
F♭ (E♮)	F	F# (or G♭**)
E♭ (D#)	E	E# (or F♮)
D♭ (C#)	D	D# (or E♭)
C♭ (or B**)	C	C# (or D♭*)

* Read as upper parallel of the upper neighbor of the alternate key.
** Read as lower parallel of the upper neighbor of the alternate key.

Ex. 1 - Matrix for determining upper or lower parallel keys

READING UPPER PARALLEL KEYS

Read the original notation a half-step higher by making a mental change of key by reading all written double flats (bb) as flats (b); flats as naturals ( ); naturals as sharps (#); and sharps as double sharps (##).

The original key and notation of C major...

will be read mentally as C# major

Ex. 2 - Upper parallel transposition

READING LOWER PARALLEL KEYS

Read the original notation a half-step lower by making a mental change of key by reading all written double sharps (X) as sharps (#), sharps as naturals ( ), naturals as flats (b) and flats as double flats(bb).

The original key and notation of C major...

will be read mentally as C♭ major

Ex. 3 - Lower parallel transposition

READING NEIGHBORING KEYS

Reading upper and lower neighboring keys involve a mental change of **key** *and* **notation** either one step above or below the written key and notation. The relationship of the written notation to the key (tonic, dominant, raised 3rd, lowered 5th, etc.), should be studied until its **"parallel"** can be easily recognized in the new key.

The difficulty of reading in neighboring keys is looking at a set of notes in *one* **key and superimposing a different set of notes in a** *different* **key above or below the written notes mentally.** These difficulties can be minimized by having a thorough knowledge of all basic scales and arpeggios, or by making a special effort to recognize them visually in musical passages. This will aid in executing their equivalents in the new key, instead of trying to read said passages on a note-by-note basis.

To read the original key and notation of C major in **upper neighbor,** mentally read the original notation in the key of D major:

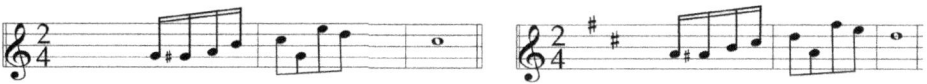

Ex. 4-Reading in upper neighboring keys

To read the original key and notation of C major in **lower neighbor,** mentally read the original notation in the key of Bb major:

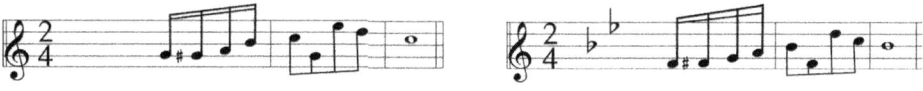

Ex. 5-Reading in lower neighboring keys

READING IN "C" CLEFS

For students familiar with "C" clefs, reading neighboring keys can be facilitated by reading the written notation of treble clef in C clefs, expressed either as alto or tenor clef.

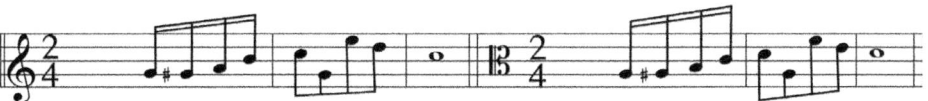

Ex. 6-Reading upper neighboring keys by reading treble clef notation in C (alto) clef

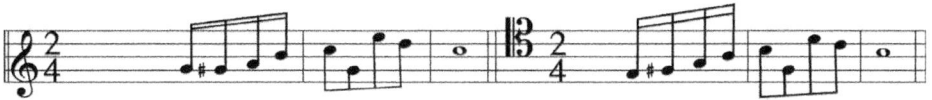

Ex. 7-Reading lower neighboring keys by reading treble clef notation in C (tenor) clef

READING F CLEFS

The treble (G clef) and bass (F clef) clefs are the most commonly known and widely used clefs in our Western system of music notation. For this reason, they are the only clefs used in *The Cyclic System of Transposition*. Students having previous experience on a bass clef instrument, piano or organ should have little or no problem reading bass clef notation. Compensatory instruction may be necessary for students who lack familiarity with the F clefs, expressed either as **bass** or **baritone clefs**.

The F clefs are used in *The Cyclic System of Transposition* to effect changes of key and pitch involving intervals of either a 3rd or 5th above the written treble clef notation without necessitating mental changes in the note/staff relationship.

To transpose treble clef notation upward by a third, mentally read treble clef notation in bass clef, as:

Ex. 8-Reading treble clef notation in bass clef

To transpose treble clef notation upward by a fifth, mentally read treble clef notation in baritone clef, as:

Ex. 9-Reading treble clef notation in baritone clef

Determining the Interval of Transposition (IOT)

All *"transposing"* instruments, except the string bass and contra bassoon, are notated in treble clef. Piccolo trumpets in Bb and A as well as sopranino trumpets in D, Eb E, F and G will sound *above* the written notation. The soprano trumpet in C will sound the *same* pitch as written, while soprano trumpets in B, Bb A, Ab and G as well as the bass trumpet will sound *below* the written notation.

The interval of transposition (IOT) for a specific instrument is determined by the interval and direction of the actual pitch sounded when third space C is written or performed.

> **Accordingly,** the sopranino trumpet in Eb is so-called because when it reads third space C, the actual sound emitted is fourth space Eb. Therefore, its IOT is a minor third *above* the written notation. Conversely, when the soprano trumpet in A reads third space C, the actual sound emitted is second space A. Therefore, its IOT is a minor third *below* the written notation.

The Cyclic System of Transposition for Trumpet

TRANSPOSITION CHART FOR COMMONLY USED TRUMPETS

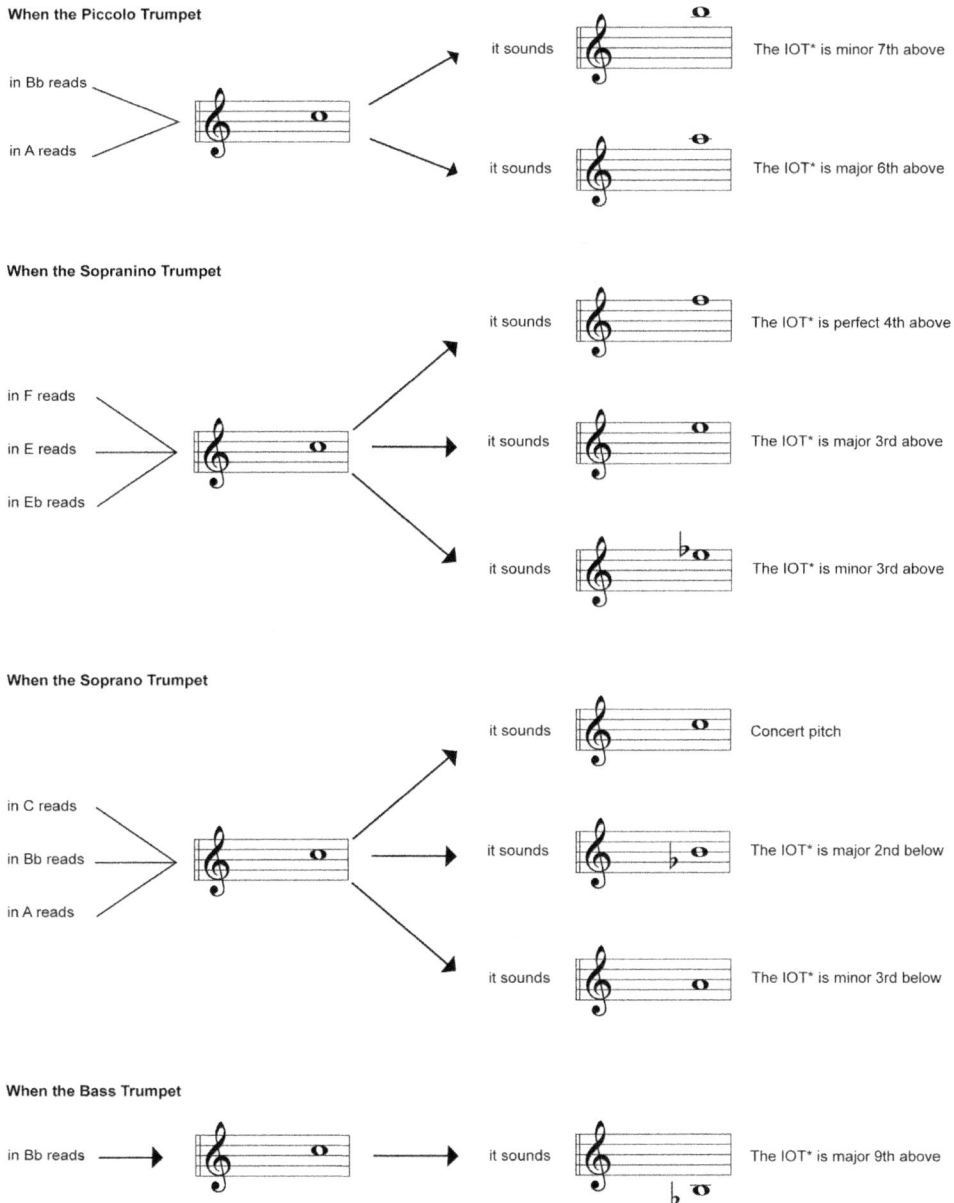

TRANSPOSITION CHART FOR COMMONLY USED TRUMPETS

Applying the Cyclic System of Transposition

It would be unreasonable to expect or require students or even professionals to own or purchase all of the trumpets listed on the foregoing chart. However, students who expect to perform in an orchestral setting must learn to read the written notation or transpose for the more commonly used trumpets that are not in their possession. The more commonly used trumpets include the Bb, A and G piccolo* trumpets, F, Eb, and D sopranino* trumpets, C, Bb and A soprano* trumpets, and the Bb bass trumpet. Although the average undergraduate student will own only a Bb soprano trumpet, the following transposition charts have been designed to accommodate trumpets of ALL pitches.

CYCLIC SYSTEM INSTRUCTION CHART

PART WRITTEN FOR:	Bb Picc.	A Picc.	Ab Picc.	G Picc.	Gb Picc.
Tpt in hand Bb Picc	As written	As lower parallel	As lower neighbor	As upper neighbor, BT**	As upper parallel, Bs***
Tpt in hand A Picc.	As upper parallel	As written	As lower parallel	As lower neighbor	As upper neighbor, BT
Tpt in hand Ab Picc	As upper neighbor	As upper parallel	As written	As lower parallel	As lower neighbor
Tpt in hand G Picc.	As lower parallel, BS	As upper neighbor	As Upper parallel	As written	As lower parallel
Tpt in hand Gb Picc	As bass clef	As lower parallel, BS	As upper neighbor	As upper parallel	As written

Ex. 10-Transpositions for Piccolo Trumpets

* It is possible to modify the pitch a half or whole step by exchanging the *"lead pipes"* of specific trumpets.
** BT =baritone clef *** BS = bass clef
****NR= not recommended

The Cyclic System of Transposition for Trumpet

PART WRITTEN FOR	F tpt	E tpt	Eb tpt	D tpt	Db tpt	C tpt
In hand, F tpt	As written	Lower parallel	Lower neighbor	Upper Neighbor, BT	Upper parallel, BT	NR****
In hand, E tpt	Upper parallel	As written	Lower parallel	Lower neighbor	Upper neighbor, BT	Upper parallel, BT
In hand, Eb tpt	Upper neighbor	Upper parallel	As written	Lower parallel	Lower neighbor	Upper neighbor, BT
In hand, D tpt	Lower parallel, BS	Upper neighbor	Upper parallel	As written	Lower parallel	Lower neighbor
In hand, Db tpt	As bass clef	Lower parallel, BS	Upper neighbor	Upper parallel	As written	Lower parallel
In hand-C tpt	Upper parallel, BS	As bass clef	Lower parallel, BS	Upper neighbor	Upper parallel	As written

Ex. 11-TRANSPOSITIONS FOR SOPRANINO TRUMPETS

---

* It is possible to modify the pitch a half or whole step by exchanging the *"lead pipes"* of specific trumpets.
** BT = baritone clef *** BS = bass clef
****NR = not recommended

WRITTEN FOR	B tpt	Bb TPT	A tpt	Ab tpt	G tpt	Gb tpt
In hand-B tpt	As written	Lower parallel	Lower neighbor	Upper neighbor, BS, 8ve lower	Upper parallel, BT, 8ve lower	NR
In hand-Bb tpt	Upper parallel	As written	Lower parallel	Lower neighbor	Upper neighbor, BS, 8ve lower	Upper parallel, BT, 8ve lower
In hand-A tpt	Upper neighbor	Upper parallel	As written	Lower parallel	Lower neighbor	Upper neighbor, BT, 8ve lower
Inhand-Ab tpt	Lower parallel, BS, 8ve lower	Upper neighbor	Upper parallel	As written	Lower parallel	Lower neighbor
In hand-G	Bass clef	Lower parallel	Upper neighbor	Upper parallel	As written	Lower parallel
In hand-Gb tpt	NR	Bass clef	Lower parallel	Upper neighbor	Upper parallel	As written
In hand-Bb Bass tpt	NR	As written	NR	NR	NR	NR

Ex. 12-TRANSPOSITIONS FOR SOPRANO AND BASS TRUMPETS

* It is possible to modify the pitch a half or whole step by exchanging the *"lead pipes"* of specific trumpets.
** BT =baritone clef *** BS = bass clef
****NR= not recommended

Interpreting Alterations

In the normal process of reading music, the performer will invariably be confronted with reading chromatic alterations. Calculating such alterations is perhaps the most perplexing problem related to the process of transposition. Perhaps the most efficient manner of transposing altered notation is by relating the function of the alteration to the note to be transposed. There are four basic functions of chromatic alterations:

1. Basic alteration-functions to resolve or embellish the pitch of a single note.
2. Minor keys-several altered notes functioning in conjunction with a major key to form a minor key.
3. Modulation-functions to effect a modulation or change of key.
4. Atonal Music—independent alterations not associated with a standard tonal key.

Once the function of the altered note (or notes) has been established, transpose the new altered notes by applying the same function when mentally reading in the new key. Remember, it is more efficient to recognize and transpose scale lines or fragments, arpeggios or chords and chromatic functions, as opposed to reading or transposing each note individually.

Perfecting the Cyclic System

It is suggested that students beginning the study of transposition use "The Art of Phrasing" section of *The Complete Method for Trumpet,* by J.B.R. Arban, to practice the fundamental principles and techniques advocated herein. Practice transposing exercises written in the key of C major without alterations at first and, as progress is made, gradually progress to keys with an increasing number of altered notes. As you become increasingly proficient in transposing in the more common keys, begin practicing music with chromatic changes. As progress is made in this sequence of practice, practice more advanced exercises as those included in *100 Studies* by Ernst Sachse, practicing in a similar manner and sequence as was done with the Arban exercises. For maximum efficiency, advanced transposition students should progress to include orchestral excerpts and studies.

The Cyclic System of Transposition has proven itself to be very effective for myself and the many students I have instructed over the years. Many of these students continued their studies and earned graduate degrees from major colleges, universities and conservatories. As a teacher or student, you are encouraged to try the system. **You'll like it ... because it *works*!**

Subject Index

A

alterations, 11, 15, 39, 41
   chromatic, 39
   independent, 39
alto clef, 13

B

baritone clef, 13, 25-26, 35, 40
bass clef, 13, 25, 33, 35, 37, 40
bass trumpet, 27, 37

C

Complete Method for Trumpet, 41
Cyclic System, 13, 41

F

F clef, 13, 25
flats, 17, 19

I

instruments, concert pitched, 10
interval of transposition, 27

L

lower parallel, 13, 17, 19, 33, 35, 37

M

major key, 39
minor key, 39
modulation, 39
music
   chromatic, 11
   tonal, 13

N

neighboring keys, 13, 21, 23
notation, 11, 13, 17, 19, 21
   written, 13, 21, 23, 27, 31

O

100 Studies, 41

P

pitches, 9-11, 13, 25, 27, 31, 35, 39

S

sharps, 17, 19
sopranino trumpets, 27, 35
soprano trumpets, 27, 31
sounding pitch, 7, 9

T

tenor clef, 23
transpose, 9-11, 31, 39
transposing instruments, 10-11, 27
transposition, 7-11, 13, 15, 17, 19, 21, 23, 25, 27, 29, 31, 33, 35, 37, 39, 41
  systems, 8, 13
  techniques, 11, 13
treble clef, 10, 13, 23, 25-27
  notation, 13, 23, 25-26
trumpets, 7-9, 11, 13, 27, 29, 31, 35, 41
  sopranino, 27
  soprano, 27
tubas, 10

U

Upper parallel, 13, 17, 33, 35, 37

W

written key, 13, 21
written pitch, 9

Printed in Great Britain
by Amazon